99 Inspiring Stories for Presentations

Inspire Your Audience & Get Your Message Through

Barry Powell

ISBN: 151979097X

ISBN-13: 978-1519790972

DEDICATION

To the woman who believed in me
when I didn't believe in myself.

Table of Contents

Introduction

"Make them care."

This is the greatest advice that the most successful public speakers will give you. Whether your audience is hundreds of business executives in a conference room, your marketing team being briefed by you, or just a few peers around you drinking cocktails on a networking event, the key to putting your message through and making an impact is to make your audience care.

Storytelling is a powerful technique that can do this.

When you just dump information onto your audience, you are not really making an impact on their hearts and minds. But, when you start telling a story, a magic thing happens: They instantly give you their full attention. They start really listening to what you are saying with their hearts and minds. And this is your chance to evoke in them some kind of emotion. Delivering your message with a funny or touching story end is the key to creating emotion and making a lasting impact in their hearts and minds.

This collection includes some of the most amazing stories ever told by famous businessmen, spiritual leaders and bestselling writers. If you are determined to improve your presentation and public speaking skills, this book is a highly recommended starting point. The stories included cover a wide range of business values to help you start practicing your storytelling skills at every opportunity.

Using stories from this collection in your presentations will help you:

- Deliver an outstanding presentation even to a tough audience
- Get your message through effectively
- Inspire and motivate others into taking the desired actions
- Start being regarded as an inspiring public speaker

You will also discover that practicing storytelling frequently, not only in presentations but in your daily conversations as well, will make you popular in your business and social circles as people will seek your company and look forward to starting a conversation with you.

Start today! Pick a story, practice at every opportunity and enjoy the benefits of being an inspiring storyteller!

How to use this book:

Let's say that you are giving a business presentation and you want to talk about stress control. Go to the table of contents and find a story about STRESS. You can include this story in your presentation. Some of the stories make really good jokes, relevant to the message you wish to get through. It is strongly recommended that you do a couple of rehearsals in advance. You will discover that including a 2-minute story in your presentation will entertain your audience and will help you get your message through more effectively.

For most of the stories I chose not to include a closing paragraph stating the moral of the story, as I believe it is obvious and, some times it's better when our mind is left unbiased to draw our own conclusions. I would love to hear your opinion about this.

If you have questions or you have some ideas that could improve this book, please contact me at barrypowellbooks@gmail.com. **To leave a review** for this book, please follow the link **http://trk.as/ymsp**

Barry Powell

"Great stories happen
to those who can tell them."

—Ira Glass

#1 ASSESSMENT: The Old Farmer's Fortune

An old farmer was working on the land with his horse. As the horse was sick, he felt compassion and decided to leave the horse loose so that it could go in the mountains where it could live free for the remainder of its life.

A neighbor from a village nearby visited, and after hearing the story he said to the farmer, "Why did you do that? Now the only horse that you had, is gone. You are so unfortunate! How will you work the land now?" The farmer said: "We shall see."

After three days, the farmer's horse came back to the farm with ten new healthy and young horses that followed the old horse.

When the village heard of the old farmer's good fortune, people stopped by the farm to congratulate him "What a good fortune!" they exclaimed. "You must be very happy now!" Again, the farmer said, "Who knows? We shall see."

The farmer had a son. One day after the horses came to the farm, the son attempted to train the wild horses, but one of them threw him down and he broke his leg. Then the villagers who stopped by thought this was a big misfortune, "Such bad luck! Your son now cannot work and you alone cannot handle all the farm's work. How will you manage? You must be really upset and sad." The farmer answered, "We shall see."

One month later, a war broke out. Soldiers arrived in the village demanding that men and all boys above a certain age come with them to be conscripted into the Emperor's army. Because of his broken leg, the old farmer's son was deemed unfit and was not chosen. "What a good fortune you have!" said the villagers. "Our young sons are marching away but yours is home with you. You must be really happy." Once more, the farmer replied: "Who knows? We shall see!" and then he headed off to work the field.

The son's broken leg eventually healed but he was left with a small limp. Again some villagers came to comment on the farmer's fortune: "Bad luck, my friend. You still have no help with the farm!" Again the farmer replied; "We shall see. Who knows?"

As it turned out, most men and boys of the village had died in that war and the farmer and his son were the only able bodied men capable of working the lands. The farmer's family became wealthy. Some villagers said to him "What a good fortune!" And again, the farmer replied, "We shall see!"

#2 ASSUMPTION MAKING: Change Your Course, Now!

A ship had been at sea in bad weather for days. As the visibility was not good because of a heavy fog, the captain stayed on the bridge to keep an eye on all directions. Suddenly the lookout on the bridge cried "I can see light far away."

The captain shouted to the signalman, "Signal the other ship: We are on a collision course. It is advisable that you change your course 30 degrees."

The signal that came back read, "You are advised to change your course 30 degrees!"

The captain said to the signalman, "Send to him: This is the ship's captain. Change your course 30 degrees immediately to avoid collision!"

"I'm a seaman second class," came the reply, "No, I repeat, you change your course immediately to avoid collision!"

The captain became furious. He said to the signalman, "Send: This is a US battleship, the second largest in the United States. I demand that you immediately change your course!" Then came the signal from the others.

"This is a lighthouse! Your call!"

#3 ASSUMPTION MAKING: A Stranger and Her Hazelnut Biscuits

At the airport, a lady waited for her flight, which was delayed. She went to the airport shop, bought a book, a hot chocolate, and a small pack containing 5 big hazelnut biscuits.

She found a seat in the lounge and started reading her book. Next to her a stranger was sitting. She did not pay any attention to him and she quickly became absorbed in her reading. She took a nut biscuit from the pack, ate it and then had a sip of her hot chocolate.

To her big surprise, the man sitting next to her calmly took one biscuit out of the pack and ate it. She was stunned! And she couldn't think of anything to say, so she nervously continued her reading.

A couple of minutes later, she picked up the third biscuit and ate it. Then the stranger calmly took the fourth biscuit and ate it. "Incredible!" she thought, even more stunned.

Then, to her amazement, the man picked up the pack and offered her the last hazelnut biscuit.

This was too much to tolerate! The woman was furious. She picked up her belongings, and walked directly to the boarding gate.

She opened her bag to find her boarding ticket, and what do you think she saw? An unopened pack of hazelnut biscuits... "If my pack is here," she thought in despair, "the other pack was his, and he tried to share."

So she realized with grief, that the only rude person, the thief in this story, was herself and not the stranger!

#4 ASSUMPTION MAKING: Big Johnny Doesn't Pay

One day, a bus driver drove off along the route with everything looking normal for the first few stops, as usual. At the next stop, a big tall guy full of muscles got on. He glared at the bus driver and said, "Big Johnny doesn't pay!" and went to the back and sat down.

Now the driver was five feet two, thin, and rather meek. He was not happy about Big Johnny's attitude, but he decided not to argue with him.

The next day Big Johnny got on again, refused to pay, saying the exact same thing and sat down. And this was repeated also the next day, and the day after, and so forth, for weeks. The bus driver started to get irritated with Big Johnny's attitude.

Finally, he would stand it no more. He signed up for karate and body building courses as well as self-defense lessons. By the end of the autumn, he had become quite confident and strong.

So on the next day, when Big Johnny got on the bus and said, "Big Johnny doesn't pay!" the driver stood up. He glared back at Big Johhny and screamed, "And why not, Mister?"

With a very surprised look on his face, Big Johnny replied, "eehhhh... Big Johnny has a bus pass!"

#5 ASSUMPTION MAKING: The Photographer and the Pilot

Tom was told that a certain plane would be waiting for him at noon at the airport.

Arriving at the spot, he saw a plane warming up just outside the hanger.

He greeted the pilot, jumped in, and without asking anything, he said "Let's go!"

So the pilot took off.

When in the air, Tom said to the pilot, "Fly low over the mountain so I can take pictures of the hill."

The pilot replied, "Why?"

John answered, "Because I'm the photographer for CBS news. I want to take some close up shots."

The pilot was silent for a moment. Then he stammered "So you are not my flying instructor?"

#6 ATTITUDE: Making a Good Light Bulb

Thomas Edison tried two thousand five hundred different materials in the process of searching for a filament for the light bulb.

None worked satisfactorily. So his young assistant complained, "So much work for nothing. We have not learnt anything so far." Edison replied with confidence,

"Really? Haven't we learned that there are two thousand five hundred elements which we cannot use to make a good light bulb?"

#7 ATTITUDE: The Greatest Baseball Player

A little boy was overheard talking to himself as he strode through his backyard, baseball cap in place and toting ball and bat.

"I'm the greatest baseball player in the world," he said with pride.

Then he tossed the ball in the air, swung and missed.

Undaunted, he picked up the ball; he threw it into the air and said to himself, "Yes, I'm the greatest player ever!"

He swung at the ball again. Again, he missed. He paused a moment to examine bat and ball carefully.

Then once again he threw the ball into the air and said, "I'm the greatest baseball player who ever lived."

He swung the bat hard and again missed the ball.

"Wow!" he exclaimed. "What a pitcher!"

#8 ATTITUDE: Bounty for Wolves

There was once a wildlife protection organization that offered a bounty of $3,000 for wolves captured alive.

Two friends, John and Jim, decided to make their fortune. So they scoured the mountain and the forest day and night, looking for wolves.

One night, as they were exhausted, they fell asleep.

Suddenly, John woke up by the sound of growls and saw that they were surrounded by a pack of nearly 20 wolves with scary black eyes, and bared teeth. From their throats, low growls rumbled.

He slowly reached over and woke Jim and said, "Jim, wake up! I think we are rich!"

#9 ATTITUDE: New Store Selling Idiots

Two men were taking a break in their soon-to-be new store. The store was not ready; only a few shelves were set up with no inventoried stock yet.

As they were both sitting on the floor, the one said to his partner "I bet any minute now, some idiot tourist is going to walk by, put his face to the window, and ask what we are selling."

No sooner were these words out of his mouth when, a man walked to the window, had a peek, and asked "Hey, what do you guys sell? This store window looks interesting."

One of the men smiled and replied sarcastically, "We are selling idiots."

Without skipping a beat, the man nodded and said, "You are doing very well, I see. Only 2 idiots left!"

#10 ATTITUDE: Thomas Edison's Laboratory

In December of 1914, a big fire completely destroyed Thomas Edison's laboratory.

Much of Edison's life's work went up in flames that night.

At the sight of the fire, Edison's son was frightened, and searched for his father. He found him, among the smoke, calmly watching the flames all over. His face was glowing as it reflected the glare of the flames.

The son was upset as he thought that his father was 67 already and everything he had was going up in flames.

The next day, Edison looked at the burned laboratory and said to his family, "I have good news for you. This disaster has a great value because all our mistakes are burned up. Thank God, we can start anew!"

#11 ATTITUDE: The Great Golfer and the Lying Woman

Robert De Vincenzo, a famous Argentine golfer, once won a tournament. He received his check, smiled for the photographers and then walked alone to the parking lot, to his car. There a young woman approached him.

She congratulated him for winning the game and then told him that she had a child that was very seriously ill, almost near death. She had lost her job and could not pay the hospital expenses and the doctor's bills.

Her story touched De Vincenzo. He took out a pen and the check, he endorsed it and then he gave it to her. "I hope this can make the baby's days better," he said as he gave her the check.

That same day, as he was having dinner in a country club, the Golf Association's vice-president sat down at his table. "Robert, I heard that you were approached by a young woman at the parking lot." The golfer nodded. "Well," said the man, "I have news for you. She lied. She has no children. She deceived you and took your money, my friend."

"You mean there is no dying child?" said De Vincenzo.

"No, there is not," said the official.

"Well, that is the best good news I have heard all week!" De Vincenzo replied.

#12 ATTITUDE: The Same Joke

One day in the village, there was a gathering of lots of people around a wise man. Most of them complained to the wise man about a problem, which, the wise man had heard again many times in the past. The wise man was silent for a moment. Then he told the villagers a joke and the whole audience roared in laughter.

After a couple of minutes, he started telling them another joke. But it was the same joke, again. When he finished, only a few of the villagers smiled.

Then he told the same joke for the third time, and no one laughed anymore.

The wise man smiled and told the villagers, "You cannot laugh at the same joke over and over. So why are you always crying about the same problem? Why are you always angry about the same problem?"

#13 CARING: The Secret of Growing Good Corn

Once there was a farmer who grew corn in his lands. Each year, his corn won the first place in the state fair.

One year, when the fair was over, a journalist asked him what the secret of his success was. The farmer revealed to the journalist that one of his success factors was that he shared seed corn with his neighbors. The journalist was surprised.

"Why do you share your best seed corn with the neighbors? Each year they are entering corn in competition with yours!" the journalist said.

"Didn't you know," said the farmer, "the wind picks up pollen from the ripening corn, then it swirls it around, from field to field. If the neighbors grow inferior corn, it is certain that cross-pollination will eventually degrade the quality of my corn. So it is smarter to help my neighbors grow good corn too, if I want to keep growing good, award-winning corn."

#14 CARING: Two Ill Men

Two men in a hospital room were seriously ill. One man had his bed next to the room's only window. Unfortunately, the other man could not move and had to be flat on his back.

One day, the man in the bed asked the other patient to describe everything that he could see outside that window.

"What lovely weather. You should see this beautiful park across the street and its lovely lake. Some ducks play on the water. There are three kids that sail their plastic boats. Now a couple walks arm in arm on a path full of red, white, and yellow flowers. In the distance you can see a great view of the city skyline."

Every day the man by the window would describe all activities in the park, and the man on the other side of the room would close his eyes and imagine the scene. That helped him feel better and be more positive about life.

Weeks passed. One month later the man by the window died in his sleep, peacefully.

A couple of days later the other man asked to be moved next to the window. The nurse made the switch and then left him alone.

Slowly and painfully, he propped himself up on one elbow. He wanted to take his first look at the park and the world outside.

But he saw no park, no children, no lake. What he saw, blew his mind.

It was a blank wall.

#15 CARING: The Most Important Question of the Test

During my last year in college, our philosophy professor gave us a test. Thirty minutes later, I had finished all questions except one, the last one. This question was totally unexpected. "What is the first name of the woman who cleans the school?"

Was this some kind of joke? I had seen the cleaning lady many times. She was tall, with dark hair, in her fifties. I had even smiled at her once or twice. But I didn't know her name. Why should I know her name? I left the question blank and handed in my paper.

One student asked the professor if this question would affect our test grade. "Absolutely," he replied.

And then he explained to us the reason why this question was so important.

"In your careers and life, you will meet many people. Each one of them is significant. You can smile at them and say "hello." Show some interest and ask them their name, who they are, their story. You may learn much more than you think."

I have never forgotten those words. I also learned that the lady's name was Rose.

#16 CHALLENGE: Japanese Fresh Fish

The Japanese have always loved fresh fish. But the waters close to Japan have not held many fish for decades.

So to find more fish, fishermen had to go further. The further they went, the more days they would spend at sea, before bringing the fish to the market. And by that time, the fish were not fresh anymore and the taste was not so good for the Japanese standards.

The installment of freezers on the boats was one solution applied by the fishing companies. The freezers would keep the fish frozen and the boats could spend even more days at sea. However, the taste of the frozen fish, again, was not as good as the taste of the fresh fish.

Then the fishing companies thought to install fish tanks. The fisherman caught the fish and stuffed them in the tanks. This way the fish were kept alive, but after a few hours they would get tired and they would stop moving. Unfortunately, the fish would not move for many days and would lose their freshness. Again, you taste the difference.

Finally, a creative mind came up with another solution to the problem.

Fishing companies put the fish in the tanks and then added a small shark to the tank! The shark ate a few fish, but most of them were in a very lively state. Because challenge is the key to maintaining vitality of mind and body!

#17 COMMON SENSE: The Mental Clinic

A group of managers and directors were being given a tour in a mental clinic.

One of the managers could not help making insulting comments about some of the patients.

After the tour, the group was introduced to the staff of the canteen.

The rude manager chatted to a man of the security staff, Sam, who was a kind ex-policeman.

"Are they all raving loonies in here, then?" asked the manager.

"Just the ones who fail the test," Sam replied.

"What test?" said the manager.

"Well," said Sam, "We take them to the bathroom and we show them a bath filled with water. Next to the bath they see a bucket, a jug and an egg-cup. Then we ask them, 'If you want to empty the bath, what is the quickest way?' "

"Oh, this is very simple, almost stupid! So the normal ones know that the right answer is the bucket, right?"

"Actually no," Sam replied. "The normal ones would say 'pull out the plug.' Should I check when there's a bed free for you?"

#18 COMMUNICATION: The Quarreling Wife and Husband

One night, a man with his wife had a big fight and then they did not speak to each other most of the night.

It was normal for them to boil in a war of silence that could last for days. This time though, the man had an important flight to catch the next morning so he needed to wake up at 5:30 AM and he was concerned about it. He was a heavy sleeper and usually his wife would wake him up, but in some cases there was a good chance he would sleep right through the alarm!

But the war of silence wasn't over and he cleverly decided to write her a post-it note while she was in the kitchen, instead of asking her to wake him up, verbally. So on the paper he wrote: "Please, wake me up at 5:30 AM or I will miss my flight." He put the note on the bed, on her pillow. Then he tucked himself in and went to bed.

When he woke up the next morning, he looked at the clock and it was 7:00 A.M.! He was furious that he had missed the flight and was preparing to scold his wife when he saw a post-it note beside his pillow, that said:

"It's 5:30 AM – get up."

#19 COMMUNICATION: The Neighbour's Wife

Tony is getting into the shower just as his wife is finishing up hers, when they hear the doorbell. The woman wraps herself in a towel and goes downstairs to open the door. It is Sam, the neighbour. Sam looks at her says, "If you drop the towel, I will give you $1000 and I will leave." The woman thought for a moment and then, she dropped her towel.

Sam stared for a few seconds, then he handed her $1000 dollars and like he said, he left. The woman wrapped back up in the towel and went back upstairs. When Tony came out of the shower he asked his wife "Who was that?"

"Ehmmm, it was Sam next door," she replies. "Great!" Tony said, "did he mention anything about the $1000 that he owes me?"

Moral of the story: If you share critical information pertaining to credit and risk with your stakeholders in time, you may be in a position to prevent avoidable exposure.

#20 COMMUNICATION: The Blind Beggar and the Advertiser

An old blind beggar was begging for money on the street corner in the rush-hour. He had a tin cup and a cardboard sign, on which someone had written: 'I am Blind. Please help me.' But no one was giving him any money.

A young woman walked past and saw the blind beggar and his sign. The woman worked in a marketing agency two blocks down the street. The advertiser took a marker-pen from her purse, turned the cardboard sign back-to-front, and wrote some words on it. Then she went on her way.

Immediately, people began leaving money into the tin cup.

The blind man was surprised. After a while, the cup was overflowing. The blind man was very curious to find out what the woman had written on his sign. So he asked somebody to tell him what the sign now said.

"It says," said the man, "It's a beautiful day and I can’t see it.”

#21 CONFIDENCE: John Rockefeller's Check

Once an entrepreneur was in debt, owing money to creditors and suppliers. Stressed as he was, he went for a walk in a park. As he was sitting on a bench with his head down, thinking of a solution that could save him bankruptcy, an old man with a strange hat approached him.

"Is something bothering you, my friend?" the old man asked. The business man told the old man about his financial problems.

After listening to him, the old man said: "I think I can help you."

He asked the entrepreneur what his name was, then took out a pen and wrote him a check which he gave to the man, saying:

"This money will help you. Let's meet again exactly in one year, right here in this park. At that time, I hope that you will be able to return the money to me."

After that, the old man walked away.

The entrepreneur took a better look at the check in his hands and was shocked. The check was for an amount of 500 thousand dollars, signed by John Rockefeller. "Rockefeller? One of the richest people in the world!" he exclaimed.

"This check can solve all of my problems in no time!" he thought. But he decided to put the check into his safe and use it only if all his other efforts failed. Just the thought that he could access these resources any time, was enough to give him strength to focus on finding smart solutions to save his business.

The return of his optimism was a great thing because it helped him close some very profitable deals. A couple of months later he had earned enough profit to get out of his debt. Then his business started making money again.

One year later, he put the check in his pocket and returned to the park. Around noon, the old man appeared again. The business man took out the check and as he was about to hand it to the old man, a nurse appeared suddenly and grabbed the old man.

"Here you are! Haven't I told you not to bother people you don't know?" She exclaimed.

"I hope he wasn't bothering you, Sir. He always runs away from the house and tells people he is John Rockefeller."

Surprised, the entrepreneur was standing there, speechless. During the whole year he was building his business, buying and selling, confident that he had half a million dollars in his safe. Suddenly he realized that it's not the money, real or imaginary, that put him out of trouble. It was his new confidence that gave him strength and motivation to achieve everything that he had now.

#22 CONFIDENCE: Who Wants $20?

A famous public speaker started off his seminar by holding up a $20 bill. He asked, "Who, in this room, would like this $20 bill?"

Many hands went up.

He said, "Good! I am going to give this $20 bill to one of you, but first, I will do this!" And he crumpled the $20 bill up.

He then asked, "Do you still want it?"

Still the hands went into the air.

"I see," he replied, "Let me try something else." And he dropped it on the floor and started to grind it with his shoe.

He picked up the crumpled, dirty bill and asked again "Now, do you still want it?" Still the hands were up in the air.

"You see my friends, no matter what I did to this bill, you will want it because its value did not decrease. It is still worth twenty dollars. No matter what I did to the money, it did not decrease in value. It is still worth $20 and you still want it. If a time comes in our lives, when we are crumpled and disappointed by the decisions we have made and the paths we have taken. A time when we will feel as though we are worth nothing. When that time comes, remember: No matter what happened or what will happen, you cannot lose your value. You are still priceless to the people that love you or depend on you. Our worth depends not on what we do, but on who we are."

#23 CREATIVE THINKING: The Lost Watch

Once a farmer lost his gold watch in his big barn. As it was not only expensive but it also had sentimental value, he spent a lot of time searching among the hay. But he gave up and asked some children playing near the barn to help him find his watch and promised a reward.

The children got inside the barn and started searching everywhere. They went through and around the entire stack of hay but no luck. They could not find the watch.

The farmer was about to give up searching for the watch, when a little boy asked to be given another chance. The farmer gave the boy permission and the boy went back to the barn.

After 20 minutes, the little boy came out holding the watch in his hand! The farmer was surprised, and asked the boy how he found the watch when the rest of them had failed.

The boy said, "All I did was to sit quietly on the ground and listen. After a while, in the silence, I heard the ticking of your watch, so I just looked for it in that direction."

#24 CREATIVE THINKING: The Height of a Skyscraper

During a physics exam, the professor asked the students to describe how they would measure the height of a skyscraper using a barometer.

One student replied, "I would tie a piece of string to the neck of the barometer. The string should be long enough. Then I would lower the barometer from the roof to the ground. The string's length plus the barometer's length will equal the skyscraper's height."

This student failed the test. The professor told him that although his answer was correct, it did not display any knowledge of physics.

The professor decided to give him a second chance. The student should provide any verbal answer that show the basic principle of physics.

"There are different ways to measure the height," he said.

"A first solution would be to take the barometer up to the roof, drop it and measure the seconds it will take to reach the ground."

"A second solution would be to observe the shadow of the sun. You could measure the barometer's height, then set it on end, then measure the length of its shadow."

"A third way would be to tie a short string to the barometer, swing it like a pendulum and count it."

"Personally, I would go with the fourth solution. I would say to the janitor, 'If you would like a nice new barometer, I will give you mine if you tell me the height of the building.'"

The student's name was Niels Bohr.

#25 CREATIVE THINKING: The Spilled Milk

During an interview, a famous scientist was asked by the reporter why he thought he was highly creative, much more than the average person, and what was it that which set him apart from others.

The scientist replied that his creativity was the result of an experience he had when he was 2 years old.

That day, he had been trying to get a bottle of milk from the refrigerator when he lost his grip of the bottle, which fell and spilled all over the floor.

"When my mother came into the kitchen and saw this messy sea of milk, she said: 'Robert, what a wonderful mess you have made here! What a huge puddle of milk! We will clean it up, do not worry but before that, would you like to get down and play in this puddle for a few minutes? Then we will find a way for you to hold the bottle better without spilling it, next time!'"

#26 CREATIVE THINKING: The Empty Box Problem

A factory once had a serious problem concerning production. Sometimes empty boxes were shipped to the clients, without the product inside.

Obviously, something went wrong in the production line. The CEO called a management meeting and they decided to hire an engineering company to solve the problem with the empty boxes.

A team of ten experts and engineers worked on this project. Six months (and 2 million dollars) later, the team came up with the solution.

They designed a device with precision scales that would weigh each box coming out of the production line. If a box weighed less than it should, a bell would ring, the line would stop and someone would walk over and remove the empty box, pressing another button when done, to re-start the line.

When the CEO read the Return on Investment statistics of the project he was very satisfied with the numbers! All the empty boxes were removed before being shipped out of the factory. No customer complaints and they were gaining market share.

A week later, he read the new weekly statistics report. He was confused.

According to the statistics, the number of defects picked up by the scales this week was zero. It should have picked up at least a dozen a day. Could this report be wrong? The engineers and other experts who were informed about the statistics, after some investigation, came back saying that the report was correct. The scales weren't picking up any defects, because simply all boxes that got to that point in the conveyor belt were good.

Even more puzzled now, the CEO went to factory and approached the precision scales.

Close to the scale, there was a big cheap plastic desk fan, blowing the empty boxes off the belt and into a bin.

"What is this?" the CEO asked.

“Oh, that,” said a worker — “Just a fan. One of the guys put it there 'cause he was tired of coming down to the line every time that bloody bell rang."

#27 CREATIVE THINKING: The Astronauts and the Pen

When a team of astronauts was sent to space, they realized that the ballpoint pens they had with them were useless, as they would leak from the refill because of low pressure and lack of gravity.

The NASA scientists decided to find a solution to this problem. They formed a team of 3 scientists to work on the solution.

One year (and $70,000) later the team presented their solution: a state of the art pen which could work at zero gravity and very low pressures and even at zero gravity.

Another team of astronauts had the same problem during their journey to space. But that group immediately came up with a $0.10 dollar solution. They used pencils.

#28 CRISIS MANAGEMENT: The Donkey in the Well

A farmer had an old donkey. One night the donkey fell into the well. The farmer heard the noise coming from the well and discovered the difficult situation that the donkey put itself into.

The farmer assessed the situation and though he felt sympathy for the donkey, he took the decision that neither the old donkey nor the well were worth the trouble of saving. Instead, he called his two sons and asked them to help him haul dirt to bury the poor animal in the well and put it out of its misery.

At first, when the donkey felt all this dirt hitting on his head, he got panicked. But as the three men continued shoveling, a smart idea struck him. Every time a shovel of dirt landed on his back, he would shake it off and step up!

And this is what he did! He would shake the dirt off and step up! Shake the dirt off and step up! He kept saying these words out loud to encourage himself.

'Shake it off and step up!'

'Shake it off and step up!'

Every blow was painful and the situation seemed really bad, but the donkey tried to stay focused, to fight panic and to keep shaking the dirt off and stepping up!

After a while the exhausted donkey managed to step over the wall of the well! What a relief! This dirt that seemed like it would bury him alive, actually helped him to survive. The donkey handled his adversity in the best possible way.

If we face our problems, refuse to give in to panic, come up with a solution and focus on the solution, then we will be in a position to handle any difficult situation in the best possible way.

#29 CRISIS MANAGEMENT: Three Fish in a Pond

Once there lived three fish in a pond. The name of the first fish was "Plan Ahead", the name of the second fish "Think Fast", and the name of the third fish "Wait and See."

One day they heard two men saying that they were going fishing in their pond the next day. They also mentioned something about casting a net.

"Plan Ahead" said, "I'm swimming down the river tonight!" and so he did.

"Think Fast" said, "I'm sure I will think of a plan on the right moment."

"Wait and See" lazily said, "I can't think about this problem now, I'll think about it tomorrow!"

The next day the two fishermen came and cast their nets. "Plan ahead", the first fish, was not in the pond. But the other two fish were caught in the net!

"Think Fast" quickly rolled his belly up and did not move, pretending to be dead. "Oh, this fish is no good!" said the man, and threw him back into the pond. But, the third fish "Wait and See" ended up in the fish market.

Because, "In times of uncertainty or danger, when the net is cast, plan ahead or plan to think fast!"

#30 CUSTOMER EXPERIENCE: The Shoe Keeper's Customer

A woman visits a shoe store for a pair of footwear and she describes her requirements to the shop keeper.

The woman returns with a pair of shoes and says to the girl:

"You should try these. This is a top brand that I recommend to anyone in need of a comfortable pair of footwear. I have been wearing these shoes for the last 5 years, they have always been the best choice for me! I am sure they will be the best choice for you too. You should buy them!"

The girl tried on the shoes, but they were not very comfortable. In fact, they hurt her toes. "They really hurt me, madam. These are not for me."

"I think you are wrong," the woman said. "Give them a little more time. They fit me so well!"

"I don't think this is it. They just don't fit my feet, they hurt."

"Listen to me, darling. According to my experience these shoes have not let anyone down. You should be more open-minded and have more patience."

"But madam, they are not at all comfortable."

"Listen, I am just trying to help and you.... Ohh, it's no use explaining any further," the old lady replied. The girl left and never returned to that store again. What customer would want advice without first being heard and understood properly?

#31 CUSTOMER EXPECTATIONS: A Creative Housekeeper

Ritz-Carlton hotel received a letter from a customer who stayed in New York with his family, wife and daughter. His letter was about the behavior of the housekeeper, which astonished him.

Having spent their day sight-seeing around the city, the family returned to their room. There, Anna, their daughter, complained that she couldn't find her teddy bear.

They searched and found the teddy bear hidden in a cupboard, with a chocolate bar clasped in its paws.

The next day, the teddy bear was missing again. The girl found it under her bed, next to another chocolate bar.

Each day of their stay, the family would go out touring and the girl could not wait to return to their room to discover the new hiding place of the teddy bear, a game with the housekeeping lady that the family never actually met.

As the man wrote in his letter, "That was the best part of our daughter's stay in your hotel!"

#32 CUSTOMER EXPERIENCE: A Little Boy Asking for a Job

A little boy named Tom entered a grocery store, and asked the store-owner if he could use the phone. The store-owner gave him permission.

The boy picked up the receiver and punched in a seven digits phone number. The store-owner observed him and listened to the conversation.

Tom: "Hello, madam, I am looking for a lawn cutting job. Are you interested in hiring me?"

Lady (at the other end of the phone line): "I am sorry, but I already have someone to cut my lawn."

Tom: "Madam, I can do this job for half the price of the person who works for you now."

Woman: "This is a good offer, but I am not interested. I am very satisfied with the person who is presently cutting my lawn." Tom: "Madam, I could even sweep your sidewalk and your curb for free. Don't you want to have the most beautiful lawn in all the neighborhood every Sunday?"

Woman: "Thank you, but as I have told you already, I am not interested."

The boy smiled and replaced the receiver. The store owner, who was listening to the conversation, walked over to the boy.

Store Owner: "Son…that's an attitude you should be proud of. I like your positive spirit and I have a job to offer you if you are interested."

Tom: "I thank you but I don't need one."

Store Owner: "Really? You were just pleading for one."

Boy: "Actually Sir, I was just checking my performance at the job I already have!"

#33 DECISION MAKING: Five Men who Got Lost in the Forest

Five men got lost in a vast forest.

They tried to find their way out.

The first man said, "I will follow my intuition and go left."

The second man said, "I will go right. I have a strong feeling about this."

The third man said, "I think I will walk back the same path we came. This should be the safest option." The fourth man said: "I think we should keep walking ahead, so I will go straight. I am sure this forest will end and I will find a village or a farm to ask for directions."

The fifth man said, "I don't know what to do. I think I will climb up this tall tree and take a better look around before I make up my mind."

So the fifth man did. While he was climbing, the other four men scattered towards their own directions. The fifth man now could see from above what was the shortest way to a village. He thought that the others should not have chosen different paths. He was wrong, though.

Each man chose his own path and gained a different experience.

The man who went left, found a long path but in the end, this led him to the town. The man who went right, had to fight a pack of wolves, but this way he learned how to survive in the forest. The man who went back, met another team of hikers and he made new friends. The man who went straight, found indeed a farm and was hosted by the family for a couple of days before leaving for the village.

#34 DECISION MAKING: Two Pebbles

In a small village, a farmer owed a lot of money to a moneylender. The moneylender offered him a deal. He would erase the farmer's debt if the farmer gave him his daughter to marry. The farmer was not happy about this deal, so he refused.

The moneylender then offered another deal. He would put into a small bag a black and a white pebble. The girl would pick one from the bag. If she picked the white one, she would marry the moneylender. If she picked the black one, she would not marry him, but the moneylender would erase the debt. But, if his daughter refused to pick a pebble, the moneylender would send the farmer to jail.

Then, the moneylender picked two pebbles up from the ground. The girl noticed that he cheated, as both pebbles were black. The old man asked her to pick.

She drew out a pebble. Without looking at it, she fumbled and let it fall on the ground among the other pebbles. "Oh, I am so clumsy, I am sorry," she said, "Never mind though! You can tell which pebble I picked by looking into the bag."

This is a very successful example of combining fast decision making and creative thinking for solving problems!

#35 DECISION MAKING: Two Employees, the Director and a Genie

A salesman, an account manager and their director were walking to lunch when they found a very old lamp.

The manager rubbed the lamp and a genie came out and said, "I will make your wish come true. One wish each. "

The salesman said "Me first! I want to be in Tahiti, sunbathing with a pina colada in my hand, surrounded by beautiful girls."

And poof! He was gone.

"Me next!" said the account manager. "I want to be in Maldives, relaxing at a spa resort together with the love of my life."

And poof! He was gone.

"OK, your turn," the genie said to the director.

The director said, "I want those two idiots back in the office as soon as I finish my lunch."

Moral of the story: It is strongly advised to hear the opinion of all the people in the meeting room, especially that of your superiors, before you are hurried into a decision.

#36 DIPLOMACY: The Two Seers

A king called in one of his two seers and asked how long he would live. "Your highness," said the seer, "You will live long enough to see all your sons' deaths." The king became furious and immediately ordered his guards to execute the seer.

He then called for the second seer, and asked him how long he would live. "Your highness," said the prophet, "You will be blessed with long life, so long that you will outlive all of your family." The king was delighted to hear this and rewarded the seer with gold.

Both seers said the same thing. But the one seer was diplomatic, the other was not.

#37 DIVERSITY: Colorful Balloons

An old man in the city center was selling colorful balloons.

To attract the attention of children, once in a while he would release a helium filled balloon into the air. The children who saw that balloon go up, would get excited and asked their parents to buy one.

While he was busy observing the crowd, a little dark boy approached him. The boy pulled his shirt. The man noticed the boy and smiled at him. “What can I do for you, little friend?” the man asked the boy. “I have a question to ask,” replied the boy. "You released a yellow balloon and it flew high. Then a red balloon, a green balloon, a white balloon. They all flew high. If you release a black balloon, would that also fly high?"

The balloon man was surprised to hear the boy’s question. Then his eyes fell on the colored skin of the body, and he realized the matter!

The man smiled with affection to the boy and replied "Son, it is not the color of the balloon; it is what's inside it that makes it go up!" and then he released a black balloon which went up as high as the other balloons, and even further.

#38 ENTREPRENEURSHIP: Radar Trap Ahead

A police officer on duty, watching for speeding motorists, parked his car every day in a hiding place and used his radar device.

One day, the policeman was surprised that every car was below the speed limit, so he investigated the matter and soon discovered the cause.

100 yards before the radar trap, there was a 12-year-old boy on the side of the road with a large cardboard sign reading 'Attention! Radar Trap Ahead.'

Then the policeman discovered the boy's accomplice. 100 yards after the radar trap, there was another boy holding a sign reading 'TIPS FOR THE HELP' and a box down at his feet which was full of change.

#39 ENTREPRENEURSHIP: The Wife's Doilies

There was once a couple married for more than 50 years. They lived happily together and they shared everything. No secrets were kept from each other. There was, however, one secret that the woman kept from the man. The wife had a small chest hidden in her closet and she asked her husband to never open it and never ask her about it.

One day, the man told the woman that he wanted to learn what was in the box. She agreed that after so many years, the secret should be finally shared, and she opened the box. Inside the man saw three crocheted doilies and a stack of money amounting to $15,000.

The woman explained. "When we were to be married," she said, "my mother advised me never to avoid fights if I wanted our marriage to be happy. She also advised me that if you ever make me angry about something, I should just keep quiet and crochet a doily."

Her husband was moved. Only three small doilies were in the chest so all those years of living together, his wife had been angry with him only three times! "This is wonderful my love! That means that I have been a perfect husband all these 50 years and that we could communicate with each other at an outstanding level! But tell me my love, where did all of this money come from?"

"Oh," she said, "this is the money I made from selling the doilies."

#40 ENTREPRENEURSHIP: The Mathematician's Son

There once lived in a village a smart professor of physics. One day, the village president told the professor: "You may be a great professor, but I have to tell you that your son does not know the value of gold or silver, and this is a shame."

The professor called the boy and asked, "Son what is more valuable – gold or silver?" The son replied "Gold, of course."

"Yes, that is the right answer. But why is it then, that the village president claims you can't tell the difference between the value of gold or silver?"

"I have a very good explanation for this," replied his son. "Every day after school, as I am on my way home, I see the village president sitting in his yard with several village elders around him. He calls me to come near and in front of everyone, he takes out a silver coin and a gold coin. He asks me to pick up the more valuable coin. I pick the silver coin. They laugh and send me home. Every day the president calls me, asks me to pick and lets me go with the silver coin in my pocket. That is why they tell you I do not know the value of gold or silver. "

"I see but... why don't you pick up the gold coin?" the professor asked.

The professor's son showed his father a jar filled with silver coins and said, "The day I pick up the gold coin, their game will stop because they will stop having fun. And I will stop making money."

#41 EXPERIENCE: Wrong Decisions

"Sir, may I ask what is the secret of your success?" a reporter asked a successful businessman.

"Two words,"

"What are these words?"

"Right decisions."

“Certainly. But could you tell me how you make right decisions?"

"One word."

"What is that word?"

"Experience."

"And how do you get experience?"

"Two words."

"Which are ...?"

"Wrong decisions."

#42 EXPERIENCE: Drawing Canaries

There once lived a rich man who loved art. As he was fond of birds, he asked a painter to draw him a canary. The man told the painter that he wanted the drawing to be breathtaking and unique. The painter accepted the job and informed the man that he should come back in two months. Two months after, the man went to the artist's studio, but he was put off again and again, until a whole year had passed.

Finally, a day came when the man visited the artist and demanded to see the artwork as he'd had enough waiting. The artist drew out his brushes and, with ease and grace, he instantly made a picture of a canary. That was the most amazing image the man had ever seen.

At first, the man was astonished; then he became angry. "You must be kidding me! It took you only one minute to draw this. Why on earth did you make me wait for a full year?" He was in a rage.

Without saying anything, the master artist opened up a closet and out fell thousands of drawings of canaries.

#43 EXPERIENCE: A Wise Man and the Lake

A old man was walking on a long path with a few followers, heading to a neighboring village and they happened to pass a lake.

As the old man was thirsty, he asked one of his companions to go and get him some water from the lake.

The man walked to the lake but when before he reached it, three bullock carts appeared and started crossing the waters of the lake. The wheels and the animals made the water very muddy.

The man saw the muddy water and decided that the old man could not drink from it. He went back to the group and told the old man what had happened and that the water in the lake was not fit to drink.

The old man said then "Let us rest." Half an hour later the old man asked the same follower to go to the lake to get him some water to drink from the lake.

The man nodded and started walking towards the lake, thinking that the old man didn't pay attention to his words. Why would he want to drink from the muddy water?

But when he reached the lake, to his surprise, he saw that the water was clear again and looked fit to drink. The wise old man knew that it would take only a little time before the mud settled to the bottom again.

#44 EXPERIENCE: One Million Dollar Mistake

The newly appointed manager was young, but ready for new challenges. Unfortunately, the first deal that he made as the department manager was a huge mistake, which led to a loss of 1 million dollars for the company.

Then the CEO called a management meeting to discuss this serious mistake that the young manager had made.

The manager explained the situation and the reason why he was led to take such a bad decision. But as he felt guilty, and thought that the CEO was about to fire him he said, "If your wish is to retire me, admitting my fault, I will accept your decision."

The CEO replied, "To retire you? In case you haven't noticed, the company has just spent 1 million dollars on your training and is not going to throw away such valuable human resources. You may return to work!"

#45 EXPERIENCE: A Turn of a Screw

Once in a factory, the production line suddenly broke down. The management team called a meeting to find a prompt solution as that was costing them millions per day. The team asked a mechanical engineer who was expert in this field and to come ASAP and to find and fix the problem. The next day, the engineer came and managed to fix the problem quickly.

Now the engineer presented a bill for $15,000. Affronted with such large sum, the CEO asked the Head of Production for more details on how the engineer managed to make the repair. The manager told him that the engineer, after examining the equipment, took out a screwdriver and turned one screw. Then the production line cranked back to life.

The CEO thought that the engineer took advantage of him and demanded to speak with him over the phone. The expert was happy to oblige. "Let me explain the bill in a few words. For turning a screw I charged $1. For knowing which screw to turn, I charged $14,999."

#46 GIVING CREDIT: The Efficient Secretary

The CEO boasted about the skills and the extraordinary efficiency of his secretary. The Vice President was impressed and very curious to find out if that was true.

So he visited the CEO's office so as to have a chance to observe his secretary while working. It seemed that she did an excellent job.

So he asked the woman "Your boss thinks very highly of you and claims that you are extremely efficient. I saw you working earlier and I can confirm this. What's your secret?"

"Not my secret, Sir," the secretary replied, "His secret."

The secretary explained that every time she did something for him, he always acknowledged and appreciated it, no matter how insignificant, no matter how small or unimportant it was. Because of his attitude, she took infinite pains with her work.

#47 GOALS: The Fisherman and the Banker

An investment banker was in a coastal village of Mexico on vacation. In a short distance away, a fisherman's boat had just docked.

The banker was impressed by the quality of the fresh fish that the fisherman caught. He greeted the fisherman and asked him why he didn't catch more fish, since there was still some free space left on the boat.

The Mexican replied that the fish was enough to support his family needs for the next couple of days.

The Banker then asked "Then how do you spend the rest of your day, if not for fishing?"

The fisherman replied, "Ahh señor, life is nice here. I fish a little, then I go home, play with my kids and take siesta with my wife. Then I take my family and we stroll into the village. I might find a few amigos there and we gather together sipping wine and playing guitar. See? I have a busy life already."

The banker then said to him "Look! I am sure you have a good life here, but I can help you have an even better life. I am an experienced business man and my advice to you is to set a goal to become more successful in your fishing business. If you spend more time fishing, you will earn more income and you will be in position to buy a bigger boat. Then you will buy a second boat, then a third boat until you will have a fleet of fishing boats. You will sell the fish not to the middleman but to the processor directly. Eventually you will manage to open your own cannery, control your product, process it and distribute it.

Then he added, "In order to manage your investments, you would need to leave this small village and move to the Capital."

The fisherman was puzzled and asked the banker: "Very complicated things! But señor, how long would these all take?"

"10-15 years," replied the banker.

"But what then?" asked the fisherman.

The banker smiled at him and said, "Now comes the best part, my friend. At the right time you will announce an IPO and you will sell your company stock to the public. If you do this, you could make millions. You will become very rich."

"Rich! And then what?"

"Then you can retire. You can move back to your village where you can sleep late, fish a little, play with your kids, take siesta with your wife, stroll into the village and enjoy the company of your amigos sipping wine and playing guitar!"

The moral of the story is: Know what your goal in life is. You may find that it is already much closer than you think.

#48 GOALS: Catching a Car

A man's dog used to sit on the side of the road waiting for cars to come around. As soon as one came, he would run down the road, barking and trying to overtake it. One day a neighbor passing by saw the scene, smiled and asked the dog's owner, "Do you think your dog is ever going to catch a car?"

The man replied, "That is not important. The most important question is if he ever caught one, what he would do with it."

Just like that dog, many of us pursue meaningless goals.

#49 HABITS: The Magic Stone

There is a legend about a magic stone that looked like a small pebble, but could turn any metal into gold. That stone was hidden among millions of pebbles that looked alike, on a certain beach. According to the legend, a man could tell if a pebble was the real stone, because the real stone would feel warm in his hand, while all other pebbles would feel cold.

Once a man sold his belongings and camped on the seashore. Next morning, he began testing pebbles.

He picked up an ordinary pebble, then threw it away if it was cold, then he picked another, threw it again. He kept repeating the process for hours. When he felt a pebble that was cold, he threw it into the sea and picked another.

He spent a whole day doing this. He went on and on this way, for weeks. Pick up a pebble. Cold. Throw it into the sea. Pick up a pebble. Cold. Throw it into the sea.

One day, eventually, he picked up a pebble which was warm. He threw it into the sea. Pick up a pebble… throw it into the sea. Suddenly he realized what he had done. He had developed such a strong habit of throwing every single pebble into the sea, that when the magic stone came along, he still threw it away.

#50 INFORMATION: Sir Arthur Conan Doyle and the Taxi Driver

One day, Sir Arthur Conan Doyle, the writer of the Sherlock Holmes book series, stepped out of a building in Paris, where he had just attended a conference. He went to the taxi-stand to hire a cab.

Before he could say a word, the driver turned to him and asked, "Where would you like to go, Mr. Doyle?" The famous author was surprised.

"Have you ever seen me before"? He asked the driver.

"No, sir, I have never seen you before," the driver replied. "But, I happened to read a story in the newspaper about you being in Paris for a conference. I picked you up from a taxi stand in front of the hotel where the conference took place. The ink spot on your right index finger is a good clue that you might be a writer. Your clothing is English and not French. So I added up all these information pieces of and I deduced that you are Arthur Conan Doyle."

"This is amazing!" Doyle exclaimed. "You are a real-life counterpart to Sherlock Holmes!"

"Oh Sir, I don't think I am such a skilled detective. I was just guessing. But there is one other thing for sure," the driver said.

"What is that?" Doyle asked.

"Your name is on the badge that you are wearing on the right side of your shirt."

#51 INITIATIVE: The Pigs Deal

A farmer had two sons. They all worked together on the farm. However, the father had been given the younger brother more responsibility. The older brother decided to ask his father why he did this.

The father did not provide a direct answer. Instead, he told him "Son, go to the Johnson's farm and ask if they have any pigs for sale."

The son left and soon returned. "Yes, they have three pigs to sell."

The father said, "Could you please go back and ask them the price?"

The son returned, "The pigs are $20 each."

The father said, "Could you ask them if they can deliver the pigs tomorrow?"

The son returned with an answer "Yes, they can."

Then, the father called the younger son. "Go to the Smith's Farm and see if they have any pigs for sale."

The younger son returned and his answer was this. "Yes, they have four pigs for $20 each, or eight pigs for $16 each. They said they can deliver tomorrow. I told Mr. Smith to deliver five pigs tomorrow unless he heard otherwise from us in the next hour. And I agreed that if we want extra pigs, we could buy them at $14 each."

The father turned to the older brother, who nodded his head, as he now realized why his father had given more responsibility to this brother.

#52 INTEGRITY: The Empty Pot

An emperor called his five sons and told them that it was time for him to choose his successor.

He said to them "I am going to give each one of you a very special seed. Go plant the seed and take care of it. One year from today, come and show me what you t have grown from this one seed. Judging from the plants that you bring, I will decide who will be the next emperor."

One year passed. The emperor gathered his five sons together and asked them to show him their pots. Four of the sons, one by one, showed their plants. Every plant was different but looked strong and healthy.

Then, the emperor asked the fifth son to approach. "Ting, he said, is this your pot?"

Poor Ting had brought an empty pot and all the kids were laughing and making fun of him.

"Be quiet!" The emperor said calmly. He looked at Ting, "What happened to your plant, Ting?"

Ting was shaking, "I am so sorry father. I took the best possible care of my seed. But, nothing grew in my pot."

"Behold your new emperor!" The emperor suddenly shouted. "The seeds that I gave you one year ago, were all boiled. They would not grow. But, all of you, except Ting, replaced the seed and you all grew different plants. Ting's honesty and innocence is the reason why I choose him today to be the new emperor!"

#53 JUDGEMENT: The Good and the Bad Wolf

A grandson visiting his Grandfather, told him that he was angry at a friend at school who had done him an injustice, "I will tell you a story about two wolves" said his Grandfather.

"Like you, sometimes, I have felt hate for some people who have taken advantage of me or treated me badly.

But you should know that hate will not hurt your enemy. Instead, it wears you down. Maybe you wish your enemy would die, but this is not going to happen if you drink poison yourself. I know exactly how these feelings are.

Imagine that two wolves live inside you. A good wolf that does no harm and will fight only if it is right to do so.

The other wolf, the bad wolf, is full of anger and bad temper. He fights everyone for no reason. His anger will change nothing. Instead, this wolf will end up having no friends or allies.

It is really hard for you to live with these two wolves inside, as they both try to control your mind."

The boy looked at his Grandfather's and asked, "Which wolf wins, Grandfather?"

The old man smiled. "The one I feed."

"Everyone has two wolves inside. The bad wolf of Greed, Guilt, Arrogance, Lies, Ego, Inferiority, Regret, Anger. And the good wolf, of Kindness, Hope, Love, Peace, Truth, Compassion and many more. Be sure that you feed the right wolf!"

#54 JUDGEMENT: Socrates' Triple Filter Test

One day in ancient Greece, a politician met Socrates at the marketplace. The man greeted Socrates and said "I want to tell you what I just heard about your friend, Agathon."

"Hold on," Socrates said. "Before you talk to me about Agathon, let's apply some filters on what you are about to say. The first filter is Truth. Are you absolutely sure that what you are about to tell me is true?"

"Actually I am not sure," the man said. "This is something I heard from Ambrosios and …"

"All right," Socrates continued. "So you do not know if what you are about to tell me is true. Let's move on to the second filter. This that you are about to tell me about Agathon, is it something good?"

"Umm, no, on the contrary…"

"Wait," Socrates continued, "So you want to tell me something bad about my friend Agathon, but you're not certain it's true. Still, there is one filter left. Let's see if your information can pass that one successfully. The third filter is Usefulness. Is what you want to tell me about my friend Agathon going to be useful to me?"

"Well, let me think about it… No... not really."

"Well," concluded Socrates, "If what you want to tell me something that is neither true, nor good, nor even useful to me, why tell it to me at all?"

#55 JUDGEMENT: The Man with the Retarded Son

A 25 year old man was travelling with his father on a train. Sitting by the window and seeing out, the man shouted…

"Dad, look those trees … how tall they are! And they are running with us?" His father smiled. Two ladies sitting nearby, looked at the 25 year old man. A minute later, he again exclaimed:

"Dad, look those clouds! They are pink and white! And they are running too!"

Now the ladies looked at each other and then the man again, with pity.

One of them could not resist and said to the old man. "I am sorry about your son. Have you taken him to see a doctor?"

The old man smiled and said…

"I did, Madam. We are just coming from a hospital in the Capital. My son was blind from birth, he just got his eyes today."

Every person you will ever meet has a story. Don't judge people before you know them. Their story might surprise you!

#56 LEADERSHIP: The Arrogant New CEO

A company hired a new CEO. This new boss was determined to rid the company of all slackers.

While taking a tour around the facilities, the CEO noticed a guy leaning on a wall. The room was full of workers and he thought that this was his chance to show everyone he meant business!

The CEO walked up the man and asked, "And how much money do you make?"

A bit surprised, the young man looked at him and replied, "I make $700 a week. Why do you ask?"

The CEO took out some cash and handed the man $700 in cash and then screamed to him, "Here! This is your last pay, now get out because you are fired!"

That was his first firing and he felt pretty good about it! He looked around and asked the workers, "Does anybody know what that slacker did here?"

With a grin, one of the workers muttered, "He's the pizza delivery guy, Sir."

#57 LEADERSHIP: Message to the Captain

A sailor informed the Captain that a message had just came for him from the admiral. The sailor handed the Captain a white envelope.

"I'd rather you read it to me," said the Captain.

"I think it's a personal letter, Sir. Perhaps you wish to read it in private. Or, it could be a secret code message. Shall I decode it for you?"

"No. Read it aloud to me," he ordered, "Unless you're embarrassed by a little flattery." He stuck his chest out a tiny bit further.

The sailor read, "You are the most arrogant, self-centered ego-maniac ever to command a ship in this country's navy."

The captain shouted, "Have that message decoded now!"

#58 LEADERSHIP: Four Monks on the Road

There was a monk named Sen, who was known for his exceptional leadership.

Three monks decided to visit the monastery where Sen lived to learn from him and they started out on their journey. Every day they would begin to argue over who should do certain chores.

On the fourth day, they met another monk who was also going in their direction. The monk joined the group. Now, this monk never complained about doing chores. Every time the other monks fought about which chore to do, this monk would volunteer to do the chore himself. On the tenth day of their journey, the other monks, inspired by his attitude, began to offer each other help with the chores.

Finally, the group arrived at the monastery. The three men asked to meet Brother Sen. The monk at the entrance laughed. "Brothers, is this some kind of joke? Brother Sen is among you!" And he pointed to the fourth man of their group.

#59 LEADERSHIP: The Sugar Habit

In the 1930s, there was a boy who liked eating desserts. He had become so addicted to eating sugar, that his mother decided to visit Gandhi. She thought that her child would listen to the leader's advice and stop his bad habit of eating sugar.

After a long journey, walking many miles and hours under the sun, they finally arrived in town and went to the place where Gandhi could usually be found.

The mother finally reached him and asked him to tell her boy to stop eating sugar because sugar was not good for his health.

Gandhi said to the woman, "I cannot tell your son that. Please bring him back in 4 weeks and I will talk to him, then."

The mother was surprised to hear this. But she could not do anything else, so she and her son returned home.

Four weeks later, she repeated the journey and talked to Gandhi again.

Gandhi remembered the woman and her son. He looked at the boy and said to him, "Boy, you should stop eating sugar. It is not good for your health."

The boy nodded his head and promised he would stop eating sugar.

The boy's mother was upset. "You could have told him this four weeks ago when I first came here. Why are you saying this now?"

Gandhi smiled and said "Woman, four weeks ago I was eating a lot of sugar myself."

#60 LEADERSHIP: Are You a Leader?

A young girl was filling out an application for college when she came across the question: Are you a leader?

She thought for a moment and then decided that she had better be totally honest. Her answer was "No."

She was afraid that because of that answer, the college would reject her application. However, one month later she received a letter back from the school that read:

"Dear Candidate,

We would like to inform you that this year we have already reviewed more than a thousand applications. To date, there will be some 1,322 new leaders attending our program next year.

We are in the pleasant position to inform you that we have accepted your application because we felt it was imperative that leaders have at least one follower."

#61 LEADERSHIP: Change for a Dollar

A young officer of the army went to a vending machine to buy a beer. He searched his pockets for change but he could not find any.

A soldier was passing by, so the officer asked the soldier "Do you have change for a dollar?"

The soldier said cheerfully, "I think I do. Wait a second, let me take a look."

The officer drew himself up stiffly. He gave the soldier a strict look and said "Is this a way to address a superior, soldier? Suppose you were in the battlefield, you would need to think faster. Now let's start all over again. Do you have change for a dollar?"

And the soldier came to attention, saluted, and replied "No, Sir!"

#62 LEARNING: A Cup of Tea

Nan-en, was a Japanese Zen master who lived during the Meiji era (late 19th century). A college professor came to town to visit Nan-en and learn what Zen is.

As they were both seated at the table, Nan-en served tea. He poured the professor's porcelain cup full, but then he kept on pouring.

The professor watched the overflow for a while. Then he could no longer restrain himself. "Master Nan-en, the cup is full. No more tea will go in!"

"Like this cup," Nan-en said, "your mind is full of your own thoughts, opinions, speculations. You cannot learn Zen unless you first empty your cup."

#63 LEVERAGE: Use All Your Strength

A young boy and his father were walking along a forest road. At some point, they came across a large tree branch on the ground in front of them. The boy asked his father, "If I try, do you think I could move that branch?"

His father replied, "I am sure you can, if you use all your strength." The boy tried his best to lift or push the branch, but he was not strong enough and he couldn't move it. He said, with disappointment, "You were wrong, dad. I can't move it."

"Try again," replied his father.

Again, the boy tried hard to push the branch. He struggled but it did not move.

"Dad, I cannot do it," said the boy.

Finally his father said, "Son, I advised you to use all your strength. You didn't. You didn't ask for my help."

#64 LIMITATIONS: Don't Believe in the Impossible

A man was on vacation in Africa. One day, he watched an old African man tying a giant elephant to a small wooden stake. The other side of the rope was tied to the front leg of the elephant. To his great surprise, he noticed that the giant elephant waited patiently and did not attempt to move or run away, even though he was big enough to pull out the stake at any moment.

Later that day, he asked an elephant trainer how such a big elephant would not make an attempt to break free. The trainer explained, "When the elephants are very young, we use the same size rope to tie them to a small wooden stake. At their age, this stake is enough to hold them. As they grow up and get stronger, they never try to escape, as they continue to believe that that little stake will still hold them.

The man was stunned. These would not try to break free because they believed it was impossible.

#65 LIMITATIONS: The Son's Letter

A young man who was in prison for a crime he had not committed, received a letter from his father who lived on a farm.

"Son, this year I'm unable to plant anything in the fields because my strength has left me and I can't dig the ground. I know if you were here, you would have helped me."

The son sent his father the following letter: "You idiot, dad, do not dig the land, haven't I told you that I have hidden the guns in different places on the ground?"

Of course the prison manager gave the letter to the police. Next day, the ground was dug by policemen, who searched for guns everywhere. But they found nothing. So the son wrote again: "Dad, now the ground has been dug up, you can plant your vegetables. I did the best I could do from here. I love you!"

So, where there's a will, there is always a way even in cases when it seems impossible to help!

#66 MAKING AN IMPACT: The Boy and the Starfish

An old man used to go to the beach every day for a stroll. One morning, after a big storm had passed, he was walking along the shore and saw that the beach littered with starfish. Everywhere you looked, you would see starfish in all directions.

Then the man noticed a small boy walking in the distance. The boy was occasionally bending down to pick up something small and then throwing throw it into the sea. At first the man thought that the boy threw pebbles. But as the boy came closer the man could see that the boy was throwing starfish, not pebbles, back to the ocean. "Good morning son! May I ask what it is that you are doing?" the man called out.

The young boy looked up.

"Throwing starfish back into the ocean. After the tide the beach is full of them and those poor creatures cannot return to the sea by themselves. When the sun gets high, most of them will die, so I am trying to save as many as I can."

The old man replied, "But there must be tens of thousands of starfish on the sand. I'm afraid son, you cannot really make much of a difference."

The boy bent down again. He picked up yet another starfish and threw it far, into the waters. Then he looked at the man, smiled and said, "It made a difference to that one!"

#67 MARKETING: Girl Scout Cookies

Markita Andrews was a miracle child with rare sales skills, who has generated more than seventy thousand dollars selling Girl Scout cookies since the age of 7.

Markita would go from door to door after school, to sell her cookies. Soon Markita transformed herself into a cookie-selling dynamo.

When Markita was invited once as a guest on a live TV show, the producer decided to give her a tough challenge.

He asked the girl to sell a dozen boxes of her cookies to another guest on the show. "Would you like to take home to your family a dozen boxes of Girl Scout cookies?" the girl asked the other guest.

"Girl Scout cookies? I don't buy any cookies!" the man replied. "Girl, I'm a Federal Penitentiary warden. Every night I put to bed more than one thousand criminals, robbers, rapists and muggers."

Unruffled, Markita quickly countered, "Sir, if you take some of these cookies, maybe you won't look so evil, angry and mean. And Sir, I think that, taking some of these cookies back for every one of your 1000 prisoners, would be a nice thing to do."

The man then wrote a check.

#68 MARKETING: A Worthless Donkey

An old man had a lazy donkey, that wasn't very smart and refused to obey the man. Soon the man decided that the animal was not worth keeping and he took the donkey to a weekly animal auction fair to sell it.

"I am selling this lazy, useless, good-for-nothing donkey!" he shouted.

An auctioneer gave his offer for six dollars, and so the donkey was sold.

A few hours later, the old man saw the auctioneer who had bought his donkey. Now he was auctioning another donkey, a good looking one.

The auctioneer shouted "Look at these strong muscles, this donkey is really strong! It will work tirelessly for hours and it will carry the heaviest loads!"

A man bid ten dollars.

"This animal is very intelligent. You can tell it by looking at his eyes and his gentle face. I am sure he would even protect your children from harm."

Another man bid twenty dollars.

The auctioneer continued praising the donkey's values and qualities and the bids started going higher and higher.

Finally, a man bid one hundred dollars. He said, "What a wonderful donkey! I was so impressed!"

He was the farmer that sold his donkey to the first auctioneer and he just bought back his own donkey.

#69 MARKETING: A Fortunate Mailing Mistake

A company hired a marketing consultant to help with a small postal mailing to the purchasing departments of hundreds of big corporations. The consultant drafted the letter and sourced the list in a spreadsheet. Thereafter, the marketing department of the company carried on the project.

One month later, the marketing consultant found out that a trainee working in the company's marketing department had changed the order of the rows in the spreadsheet, by sorting only the company name column and not all the columns together.

As a result, every letter (about 500) was sent to the wrong address, at the headquarters of another corporation.

Interestingly, the marketing department reported a particularly high response. They investigated the matter and found out that this mailing mistake was the cause. An unusually high percentage of the sales letters were opened and read, apparently due to the irresistible temptation of reading another company's mail!

#70 OPEN MINDEDNESS: The Preacher on the Roof

The preacher of the parish near the village is about to lock the door and return home, when a rainstorm starts. The rainstorm grows stronger every minute. The preacher decides to wait for a while inside the parish office until the rain is over. But the rain only grows stronger and after a few hours the parish house becomes flooded. The water rises and the preacher climbs to the roof and starts praying.

"Lord, please save me so I can continue preaching your gospel."

That moment, a coast guard rescue party floats by in a rowboat.

"Come down now, get into the boat."

"No sir, I will stay here," replied the preacher, "I am sure that my Lord will stop the rain and save me."

An hour later, a second boat approaches the parish, when the water is close to the roof. "Sir, get in quickly."

"Thank you but I will stay here. The Lord will provide. I am certain that the rain will stop any minute." A couple of hours later the roof is almost completely under water. The preacher is now clinging to the satellite dish on the top of the roof.

A helicopter approaches the roof.

“Sir, grab on to the line. We will pull you up,” a voice is heard on a loudspeaker. "No please go, I'm all right. My Lord will provide sanctuary," says the preacher, as he looks heavenward.

After the helicopter flew away, lightning hits the satellite dish and the preacher is killed. He arrives, furious at the Pearly Gates.

"Why did this happen?" he shouts. "I thought the Lord would provide!" Then he hears a thunderous voice.

"Gimmie a break, pal. I sent you 2 boats and a chopper."

#71 OPPORTUNITIES: The Obstacle on the Roadway

Once the mayor of a small village had a boulder placed in the middle of the roadway. Then, he hid himself behind a tree and watched the villagers passing by. He wanted to see if any of them would attempt to remove the big rock. But no one seemed to care about it.

Even some members of the council came by and simply walked around the rock. Some villagers loudly blamed the mayor for not keeping the roads clear, however none did anything to get the rock out of the way.

Then, an old peasant came along, carrying a load of vegetables. When the peasant approached the rock, he laid down his burden and tried to move it to the side. He struggled for a while, and he finally succeeded. Afterwards he picked up his vegetables, and was about to continue his way, when he noticed a purse lying on the ground, where the boulder had been placed. He opened the purse and found inside several gold coins and a note from the mayor reading that the gold was for the person who removed the boulder.

Every obstacle presents an opportunity to improve our condition!

#72 OPPORTUNITIES: Catching the Bull's tail

A young man wanted to marry the farmer's young daughter so he went to his house to ask his permission.

The farmer said to him "Son, I will give you my daughter if you can do one thing. We shall go outside to my field and I'm going to release three bulls, one at a time. All you have to do is catch the tail of any one of them. If you can do that, you have my permission to marry my daughter."

The man agreed and they went outside in the field.

The farmer opened the barn door and a huge bull came out. That bull was the meanest looking bull he had ever seen. So he decided to skip the first bull, thinking that the other two bulls would likely be a better choice than the first one. So he let the bull pass through and the farmer opened the barn door again.

Contrary to his expectations, the second bull was even bigger than the first one. There was no way he could get anywhere near this monster, let alone catch his tail. The man thought that the last bull had to be a better choice. Again, he let the bull pass through.

The farmer opened the door for the third time. A smile came across the young man's face. The bull was old and weak. "I'll go for this one," said the man. As the bull was running by, he positioned himself just right and at the right moment he jumped and threw his hands to grab the bull's tail.

But, alas…That old bull had no tail.

#73 OPPORTUNITIES: I Don't Have an Email Address

A young unemployed man heard that there was a job opening for the position of "Office Boy" at a big company and he went to their HR department to apply for it.

After a very short interview, the HR administrator said:

"You are hired! I will send you the application to fill out, so you start on Monday. What is your email address?"

The man said "Madam, I don't have an email address. I don't have a computer either."

Surprised to hear this, the personnel manager said "I find this unacceptable. Everyone has an email. We live in a world of technology," said the woman and she continued, "I am sorry but you cannot have the job. Go and learn how to set up an email account."

The man left in despair. He had only $10 in his pocket. He could not decide what to do next.

Finally he came up with an idea. He entered a supermarket, bought a 10 kg tomato crate and then he sold the tomatoes door to door. In less than 1 hour he doubled his capital. He did the same thing 3 more times and when he finished he returned home with $80 USD. The man repeated this business the next day and the day after, and so forth. Every day his money doubled or tripled. In time, he bought a cart, then a truck, then his own fleet of trucks.

Five years later, that man had become one of the biggest food retailers. One day he decided to have a life insurance policy and went to an insurance company. After a long conversation with the insurance broker, the latter asked him his email to send him the contract in digital form. The man replied: "I don't have an email."

The broker was surprised to hear that. "You don't have an email, and yet you have built an empire. Do you imagine what you could be today if you had an email?"

The man paused for a while, and replied: "An office boy!"

Don't be discouraged if you have bad luck today. Better opportunities are always waiting ahead.

#74 PERSISTENCE: Dig a Little Deeper

Two brothers sold all their belongings and went prospecting for gold. After months of hard work, they discovered a vein of gold ore, staked a claim, and started the business of getting the gold ore out of the mine.

A couple of months later and to their big disappointment, the vein of gold ore disappeared! The brothers continued to pick away, with no success. In the end they gave up. They sold their equipment and their claim rights for a few hundred dollars, and took the train back home.

Now the claim was bought by a clever man who hired an engineer to take a look at the mine. The engineer examined the rock strata and advised the man to continue digging in the same spot where the brothers had left off. Indeed, four feet deeper, the man struck gold. Just a little deeper than the depth those brothers had stopped.

Had they been more persistent, the brothers would have been millionaires themselves.

#75 PERSISTENCE: The Girl's Advice to the Salesman

A young salesman came to a neighborhood to sell his product, a professional carpet cleaning foam spray. He knocked on the door of the first house. A little girl opened the door.

"Hey, little girl! Is your mom home? I have an amazing product to show her."

The girl called her mom.

The woman saw the salesman and quickly said, "Thank you, Sir, but we don't need really anything."

Hearing this, the man sighed and said "Please Madam, at least let me show you the product. I haven't been able to sell anything today. Please."

Then the girl looked at him and said "Hey mister, how many doors have you knocked on, today?"

The salesman answered, "Around 30."

The girl continued "Do you know that Walt Disney was turned down 303 times before Disneyland got financing? Do you know that John Creasy was rejected 750 times before he became a famous novelist? Do you know that Colonel Sanders spent two years driving across all states asking restaurant owners to buy his chicken recipe and was turned down 1,010 times?"

The salesman remained silent.

#76 PERSISTENCE: Frog in a Milk Pail

One day at a farm, a frog decided to investigate the cellar in the yard.

He hopped through the open door and down the staircase, curious to see what was inside. But as it was somewhat dark, he stumbled and he fell into a small milk pail which was filled with fresh milk.

He attempted to reach the top of the pail but the sides were too high. He stretched his feet to touch the bottom of the pail but found it too deep. He didn't want to give up, so soon so he continued to swim in the milk and struggle.

He kicked in the milk again and again and squirmed continuously. Half an hour later, all the churning had turned the milk into solid butter.

So the frog could now step on the butter, reach the sides of the pail and get out of it!

"Never Give Up!"

#77 POSITIVE THINKING: The Optimist and Pessimist Twins

A family had two children, which were identical twins. One child had a very optimist personality. "Today is a great day!" he would say often. The other twin had a very pessimist attitude. "What an awful day!" he would say.

Their parents got worried about the extreme difference of their attitude and they brought a psychologist in to examine the children.

The doctor suggested an experiment that would give him the opportunity to study their personalities.

"Next week, on their birthday, put the twins in separate rooms and give each one a gift. To the pessimist child give a huge box filled with the best toys you can afford. To the optimist child give a box of manure,said the psychologist to the parents.The parents followed his instructions and on their birthday, each twin was in his own room with a box. The doctor and the parents waited outside.

They heard the pessimist twin audibly complaining: "The color of this ipad sucks! That game is so boring! I didn't want a model train, I wanted a plane! My friend Tom's backpack has a better looking design than this one here." Then the parents and the doctor peeked on the optimist twin.

They saw him giggling. He was gleefully throwing the manure up in the air. "You can't fool me! With all this manure here, there's gotta be a pony!"

Sometimes, being optimistic is the only thing you can do in the moment.

#78 POSITIVE THINKING: A Woman and her Hair

One morning a breast cancer patient, a woman in her 40's, woke up and looked in the mirror. On her head there were only three hairs. She had lost almost all her hair while undergoing chemotherapy treatments.

She said, "Well, I think today I will braid my hair."

So she did, she went to work and she had a lovely day.

The next morning when she woke up and looked in the mirror, she saw that now on her head there were only two hairs.

She said, "Hmm, I think today I will part my hair down the middle."

So she did , she went to work and she had a wonderful day.

The next morning she woke up, looked in the mirror and saw that on her head there was only one hair.

"I think today I am going to wear my hair in a pony tail."

So she did, she went to work and she had a really fun day.

The next morning when she woke up she noticed that on her head there wasn't a single hair.

"Great!" she exclaimed, "I don't have to fix my hair today!"

#79 POSITIVE THINKING: The Frogs on a Running Competition

Once a bunch of frogs decided to go on a running competition. The frog that would reach the top of the tower first would be the winner. A big crowd gathered around to watch this race and cheer on the contestants.

The tower was very high, so almost anyone in the crowd didn't really believe that the frogs could reach the top of it.

During the race, you could hear the crowd saying:

"No way, this is too difficult!"

"They will not succeed. Not a chance!"

"They must be stupid to believe that they can make it to the top."

The frogs could hear the crowd. Finally, one by one, the frogs abandoned the game.

Some of them continued to struggle and managed to climb higher and higher.

"They will not make it, this is way too difficult," the crowd continued.

So even those persistent frogs got tired and gave up. In the end, there was only one frog that wouldn't give up. The little frog struggled to climb higher and after a huge effort, he was the only one to reach the top.

A frog asked the winner how he had found all this strength to make it to the top.

The winner did not respond. It turned out that the winner was deaf.

Don't listen to people's opinions. Nothing is impossible, if YOU believe you can achieve it.

#80 PRIORITISATION: Is this Jar Full?

A teacher told his class that he would like to give them a lesson about their priorities in life. So he took a big glass jar and he put it on the table.

Then he took out a bag full of medium-sized rocks. He put the rocks inside the jar until they had filled it to the top.

Then the teacher asked, "Is this jar full?"

"Yes," everyone shouted.

"Really?" exclaimed the teacher and then he took out another bag full of gravel. He dumped the gravel into the jar until all empty spaces had been filled. Then, he asked again, "Is this jar full?"

Some of the children nodded their head yes.

Then the teacher pulled out a bag full of sand and he dumped the sand into the jar. Once more he asked "Is the jar full now?"

This time a pupil mumbled "Probably not."

"Good," the teacher said. He then took a pitcher of water and dumped the water into the jar until it was full.

He asked again, "Is the jar full now?"

"Yes." All children shouted.

"If I had started filling the jar with the water, then the sand, then the gravel, would I have ever gotten the rocks in? The children replied "No."

"Exactly! If you put the sand or the gravel into the jar first, then there is no room for the rocks," the teacher said. And he continued:

"In your life, never forget this.

If you spend your energy and your time trying to manage the small stuff, there will be no room for the things that matter, your life goals, the values that are most important to you. What are your goals? Play with your children? Make your partner happy? Enjoy a stress-free life? Work on these goals, first. There will always be time to go to work or clean the house. But you have to take care of your main goals first, the rocks. Set your priorities. The rest is just sand."

#81 PROCRASTINATION: Diagnosed with Cancer

Before Anthony Burgess become a famous author in 40s, he was diagnosed with a brain tumor and informed by the doctors that he had only one year to live. At the time Burgess was broke and thought that he had nothing to leave behind for this wife, Lynne.

Burgess always knew that he had a talent for writing. He thought it would be a good idea to publish a novel so as to leave royalties behind for Lynne. One year should be enough, he thought. So he put a piece of paper into a typewriter and began writing. Of course he knew that his novel was very likely to be rejected by the publishers but at the time he couldn't think of anything else to do.

"It was January of 1960," he said, "and according to the prognosis, I had a winter and spring and summer to live through, and would die with the fall of the leaf."

Burgess was focused and wrote energetically from early in the morning until late night. Before the year was through, he finished five and a half novels.

Contrary to the doctors' predictions, his cancer went into remission and when that year was over Burgess did not die. The tumor disappeared altogether. This is how Burgess, who is best known *for A Clock-work Orange,* begun his long and successful career as a novelist. Over the years that followed, he wrote more than 70 novels. Without the death sentence from his disease, he may not have started writing, at all.

Like Anthony Burgess, many of us hide an extraordinary talent but most of the time we never start working on it. What would you do if you, like Burgess, had just a year to live? Would you live differently? Would you try to discover your full potential before it would be too late?

#82 PRODUCTIVITY: The Busy Woodcutter

Once a strong woodcutter was hired by a timber merchant.

The woodcutter was very enthusiastic about his new job and was determined to make his best effort.

The boss gave him an axe and took him to the area where he would work.

The first day, the woodcutter cut 20 trees down.

His boss was impressed. "Keep up the good work," he said.

Next day the woodcutter tried harder. But this time he could only cut 17 trees down. The third day, even though he tried as hard, he only brought down 15 trees. Day after day, the woodcutter would bring less and less trees.

The woodcutter was confused and sad. He went to the boss to apologize for his bad performance. He said that although he worked really hard, the results were disappointing.

His boss was silent for a moment and then he asked "When did you sharpen your axe for the last time?"

"Sharpen? I had no time to sharpen my axe. I have been very busy cutting trees."

#83 PRODUCTIVITY: The Horse Shoe

A man was traveling on his horse to his village. He decided to stop for a while to have a meal in a tavern. The stable boy said to him "I noticed the shoe on your horse is missing a nail. I could replace it, if you want."

"I am in a rush" the man replied. I will have it fixed when I get home."

The man had his meal and then he continued his way. Some hours later, he stopped to feed his horse. A man at the stable said "Sir, your horse is missing a nail on its shoe. Would you like me to replace it?"

"Thank you, but I'm in a rush and I need to get home quickly" the man said.

And he left.

A few miles later, the horse's shoe came off. The man had to walk all the way back to the last stable, get a horseshoe, return to his horse and replace the horseshoe, before he could continue his way home.

Not being proactive, the man lost three hours while the stable man would have replaced the horseshoe within 3 minutes.

#84 QUALITY: The Carpenter's House

An elderly carpenter was about to retire. He told his employer-contractor of his plans to leave the house building business and live a more leisurely life with his wife, enjoying his extended family.

He would miss the paycheck, but he needed to retire. They could get by. His contractor was sorry to see his good worker go. He asked the carpenter to build just one more house before retiring. The carpenter accepted, even though he didn't really want to do so. His heart was not in his work anymore. He put in a half-hearted effort, taking shortcuts and using inferior building materials. The quality of the finished building was much below his usual standards.

When the project finished, the contractor came to see the house. He took a look around, then he took out the front-door key and handed it to the contractor. "My friend, this house is yours. This is my gift to you as a thank you for all these years of hard work." The contractor said.

The old man was shocked and embarrassed. If only he had known, things would have been done in a different way. He would have taken care of every detail and this house would be the most beautiful house that he'd ever built.

Like the old carpenter, many of us do not give the job our best effort. Then we find ourselves living in the poor quality house we have built.

#85 READINESS: A Job Interview Test

A company announced a job opening for the position of a telegraph operator. Two days after, ten applicants were waiting in the large, noisy hall in front of the personnel manager's office for a job interview.

A young man was among them. Like the others, he filled out a form that he was given and sat down to wait. He saw secretaries and clerks coming and going and heard a telegraph clacking away in the background.

A couple of minutes later, this man stood up, crossed the room and walked to the door of the manager's office. He knocked on the door, then walked right in.

The other applicants were shocked by his rude attitude. They talked among themselves, all agreeing that this man would be definitely disqualified even before his interview started.

Ten minutes passed and the man came out of the office, escorted by the personnel manager, who announced:

"Thank you for coming. The position has just been filled."

The applicants were confused and one man spoke up, "Sir, we don't understand this. All of us have been waiting much longer than him, yet we never had a chance of an interview."

The manager replied "Yes, indeed, all of you have been sitting here for more than an hour. All this time, the telegraph has been ticking out one message: "Dear applicant, come right in so we can start the interview."

#86 STATUS QUO: The Five Monkeys Experiment

In the 1980s an experiment on monkeys was made by a researcher who conducted a study on social dynamics. The researcher put five monkeys in a huge cage. At the top of the cage, he placed a bunch of bananas.

Then a ladder was placed inside the cage, leading to the bananas.

The monkeys saw the bananas and sent one of them up to get them.

When the monkey got to the top and reached for the bananas, the scientist threw a stream of cold water on the monkey's face. Caught by surprise, the monkey scurried down the ladder. Then, the scientist threw cold water on all the monkeys.

A little cold water in the face didn't entirely stifle their ambition, so a few minutes later, the monkeys sent another one up the ladder. Again the scientist threw cold water on the monkey and the monkey quickly climbed down the ladder. Once more, the cold water treatment was repeated for all the monkeys.

Ten minutes later a third monkey attempted to climb the ladder. But the other monkeys, remembering the punishment that follows, beat up the ambitious monkey and didn't let him climb up.

A few days later, the scientist removed one of the five monkeys and introduced a new monkey to the group.

The new monkey saw the bananas and naturally, attempted to climb the ladder. The original four monkeys grabbed him and beat him up. Then a second monkey was replaced with a new monkey.

Again, the new monkey attempted to climb up and the three original monkeys together with the first new monkey grabbed him and beat him up. That was impressive because the first new monkey was never given the cold water treatment, but he behaved like the other members of the group.

Gradually, all monkeys were replaced with new ones. The new monkeys continued the same treatment of any monkey who tried to reach the bananas. They would pull him off and beat him up, despite the fact that none of them experienced the cold water treatment. In the end, all the monkeys learned that they should never go for the bananas.

This experiment describes perfectly how our society often reacts, when someone attempts to break the rules and change things.

#87 STRATEGY: Judo Lessons

A 9-year-old boy who had lost his right arm in a car accident, decided to take judo lessons.

His teacher was an old Japanese judo master who decided to teach the kid one move only. After a few lessons the boy said to him "Master, shouldn't I be learning more moves?" "No. This only move you know is the only move you'll ever need to know," he replied.

Six months later, the boy had his first tournament. To everyone's surprise, the boy won the first three matches and got in the finals.

The other boy, his opponent, was bigger and stronger than him. Everyone thought that the boy had no chance to win. The match begun and the opponent, indeed seemed much more experienced than the little boy. Suddenly the opponent dropped his guard, which was a critical mistake. The boy used the only move he knew to pin him and won the tournament.

Later, the Master told the boy:

"Son, you won for two reasons," the Master answered, "First, after six months' hard practice you have almost mastered one of the most difficult throws. And second, the only known defense for that move is for your opponent to grab your right arm."

And this is how the boy's biggest weakness turned into his biggest strength!

#88 STRESS: A Glass of Water

A professor raised his glass of water in front of the students.

"How heavy is this glass of water, you think?" he asked with a smile. The students' answers ranged from 10 oz to 20 oz.

"Okay. Now, could one of you come here and help me hold the glass?"

A girl walked to her table and held the glass.

After a few minutes, the girl said, "Sir, I am tired, is it ok to leave the glass on the table now?"

The professor smiled, nodded yes and said to the students, "Imagine if you have to hold this glass for an hour or even a day! Would you think now that 10 or 20 oz weight too little?

"No," all students answered.

"Exactly! Hold it too long and you will only hurt yourself. Always remember to put the glass down several times a day," said the teacher.

"The weight of a glass filled with water does not change, but the longer you hold it, the heavier it becomes. Our worries and stresses are like this glass of water. Think about them for a moment and nothing happens. Think about them longer and they begin to hurt. Think about them all day long and you will only feel panic making you unable to do anything else."

"Do not carry your burdens all day long, from morning to night. Remember to put your burdens down as often as you can. Remember to put the glass down!"

#89 SUCCESS: The Shoes Salesmen

Two shoe salesmen were sent to Africa to find out if there was a market potential for shoes.

The first man came back and reported "There is are no business opportunities there. Everybody is poor and no one wears shoes."

The second man reported: "We just found a great business opportunity. This market has a huge growth potential! No one wears shoes!"

So, when confronted with a challenge, which salesman are you?

#90 SUCCESS: The Chicken and the Bull

A chicken was chatting with a bull. "How nice it would be if I could climb up this tree and sit on its branch," sighed the chicken, "But I don't have the energy to do it."

The bull looked at the chicken and said "Perhaps if you nibble on my droppings you will get stronger, because they are packed with nutrients."

The chicken did so and after a while felt strong enough to climb and reach the lowest branch of the tree. The next day, it ate some more dung and was able to reach a higher branch.

Getting stronger and stronger, three days later, the chicken successfully climbed to the top of the tree and sat on a branch. Soon he was spotted by the farmer, who mistook the chicken for a wild turkey and shot the chicken out of the tree.

Because bullshit might help you get to the top, but it won't keep you there.

#91 SUCCESS: Socrates' Secret to Success

Once a man asked Socrates what the secret to success was. Socrates asked the man to meet him the next morning and join him for his usual morning bath in the river. When the two men met, they got in the river and walked deeper. When the water was up on their neck, Socrates took the young man by surprise and dunked his head into the water. The man struggled to get his head out of water but Socrates kept him steadily until the man's face started turning blue.

A few moments later Socrates released his head and the man finally got out of water, gasped and took a deep breath of air.

"Why did you do that?" the man shouted.

Socrates asked: "When you were in the water, what did you want the most?"

"Air," the boy replied.

Socrates said: "You asked me the secret to success. There is only one secret. When you want success as badly as you wanted the air, then you will get it."

Indeed, if our desire is weak it will not produce great results. We need to have a burning desire to reach success.

#92 SUCCESS: Schwarzenegger's Success Story

We are what we think we are. You can't be it, if you can't see it. Your life is limited to your vision. If you want to change your life, you must change your vision of your life.

In the '70s, Arnold Schwarzenegger had reached the peak of his bodybuilding career and then decided to retire. Back then he was not as famous as now. In 1976, a journalist asked him:

"Now that you have retired from the bodybuilding scene, what do you plan to do next?"

Schwarzenegger smiled at him and calmly replied: "I'm going to be a movie star in Hollywood."

The report was surprised and rather amused by Schwarzenegger's plans. He couldn't imagine how this huge body builder with his poor English and his Austrian accent could hope to a Hollywood movie star.

“And how do you plan to make this dream come true”? the reporter asked.

"The same way I became the most famous body builder in the world. I will create a vision of who I want to be, and then I will start living like that person in my mind as if it were already true."

Sounds simplistic and childish, right? Well, it worked for Arnold!

At first all of the agencies rejected him because of his over-sized body and his accent. Let alone, that his surname was impossible for an American to pronounce. But in the end, Schwarzenegger reached his goal and became one of the most famous and highest paid movie stars in Hollywood! And after that, his next goal, a political career, was also accomplished when he was elected Governor of California.

Just to know, Arnold’s family wasn’t supportive at first. They wanted him to be a police officer like his father, or play a “normal” sport like soccer instead of pursuing a bodybuilding career. Arnold had to go against what others wanted for him so that he could discover his own path of success.

Remember: "If you can see it, you can be it."

#93 SUCCESS: Sitting on His Talent

There was once a pianist who worked in a bar and played there every night.

One night, a patron asked him to sing.

The man said, "I don't sing."

But the man was persistent. He told the bar's owner "I come here almost every night, you know it. I'm tired of listening to the piano. Tell that guy to sing!"

The owner shouted across the room, "Hey Nat! Customers want you to sing. If you want to get paid tonight, sing a song."

So, he did. He sang a song. The pianist who had never sung in public sang a song for the very first time. That night the patrons of the bar heard the best ever version of the song "Mona Lisa", sung by Nat King Cole!

Because he had to sing, Nat discovered that he had a talent he was sitting on! He would have lived his life as a no-name piano player if somebody didn't make him to sing. Cole became one of the best-known singers of the 20th century in America.

#94 TAKING RISK: A River Full of Crocodiles

A king once decided that it was time for his daughter to get married. He held an event to find the most brave man in the kingdom.

Several princes and hundreds of villagers gathered at the event.

At last, the king announced the competition, "I wish to find who among you is the bravest of all. So I have a dangerous mission for you. This river in front of you if full of crocodiles. The one who swims across and reaches the other side will marry my daughter."

The princes looked at each other, then at the river then at each other again. All of them hesitated to encounter such great danger and were not willing to swim.

Suddenly, the water splashed! A prince jumped in the waters and started swimming like crazy.

The masses were screaming in excitement. The man swam across fast and reached the other side.

The king was delighted to see such a brave man, sent a boat to bring him back and ordered his servants to begin the celebrations. The king approached the man and asked him to address the people.

The man agreed and quickly addressed, "First… I would like to know who had pushed and thrown me into the river?"

Sometimes circumstances force us to "jump into deep waters" and take risks that we wouldn't take otherwise. But this adventure may lead us to great opportunities, in the end!

#95 TAKING RISK: The Burning Hut

During a sea storm, a ship sank and the sole survivor was washed up on the beach of a very small island.

The castaway gathered all the pieces of the wreckage that had also washed up on the beach and used the driftwood to build a little hut where he could sleep and store his few possessions.

Each day, he prayed for help and each day he scanned the horizon wishing desperately to see a ship. But none was forthcoming.

One day, he saw a ship far on the horizon. He burnt some driftwood to make a fire and the smoke rolled up to the sky. But the smoke was hardly visible from such a distance, so no one in the ship noticed it.

Then, one month later, he saw another ship far away. He burned more wood this time. Still no one saw his fire and the ship disappeared over the horizon.

Weeks after that, a third ship appeared. Finally, he decided to take a big risk. He burned his whole hut, thinking that the heavy smoke would roll up to the sky and would be visible by the men on the ship.

Early next morning, he awoke to the site of a ship anchored near the island.

#96 TEAMWORK: Buster and His Friends

A traveler drove his car into a ditch near a farm. The farmer who had seen the car, came with his horse to help pull the car out of the ditch.

The horse's name was Buster.

He hitched the horse up to the car and shouted, "Let's go Bonnie! Pull!" The horse didn't move.

The farmer then yelled, "Let's go Kiko! Pull!" Again, the horse didn't move.

Once more the farmer shouted "Let's go Rudy! Pull!" Nothing happened.

Then the farmer said, "Let's go Buster! Pull!" And the horse moved and dragged the vehicle out of the ditch.

The man thanked the farmer, but being very curious he said "You called your horse three times by the wrong name. Why did you do that?"

The farmer laughed and said, "Oh, Buster is a blind old horse. If he thought he was the only one pulling, he wouldn't even try!"

#97 TEAMWORK: Finding Your Balloon

All employees of a company were attending a seminar on productivity. 60 people, in total, were in the conference room.

After the break, the trainer invited the attendants to do a group activity.

He gave each attendant a balloon and asked them to write their name on it with a marker. Then all the balloons were collected and taken to another room.

Then the trainer asked the attendants to go into the other room and find the balloon that had their name on, within 5 minutes.

Everyone was frantically searching for the balloon with their name on, colliding with each other, pushing each other, in utter chaos.

When the time was up, only a few of them had found their balloon.

Now, the trainer asked them to do the same, but with team work. They made three groups. A man in each group picked a balloon, read the name written on it and gave it to the right person. This time everyone had their balloon within three minutes.

#98 TRUST: The Frightening Air Plane Experience

In a long flight from Hong Kong to New York, the passengers heard the stewardess' calm voice saying that all passengers should remain in their seats.

Then, after a while, a calm voice said, "We are expecting a little turbulence. Please be sure that your seat belt is fastened. We will not be serving beverages until further notice."

Then the passengers could see that they were flying through a storm. Thunder was heard together with the roar of the engines, while lightning flashed in the dark every few minutes.

Later, the stewardess announced "Unfortunately we all have to be patient for the storm to be over, before we can be able to serve the meal."

A man sitting next to little girl, was scared to death and was experiencing a panic attack. Then, the man turned his head and saw that the girl next to him was calmly reading a book.

The girl smiled to the man. “Don’t be afraid, Mister” she said to him.

“How can you be so calm when we are flying through a terrible storm like this? Aren’t you afraid?”

The girl smiled and replied, "Sir, the pilot is my dad and he is taking me home.”

#99 VISION: Thinking Ahead of His Time

In 1914, a businessman announced a minimum $5.00/day pay for all eligible employees. That was double the day wage for most of the workers.

Moreover, he decided to decrease the work day from nine hours a day to eight. He said that his intention was to improve the quality of his workers' life.

Next morning the press, including "The Wall Street Journal" characterized the businessman's move as reckless and irresponsible. The stakeholders were not happy, either. But, this man proceeded with the execution of his decisions.

That businessman was Henry Ford. Having increased employee satisfaction and retention, he was able to hire the best engineers. As the productivity across the company increased dramatically, his company's profit doubled from $30 to $60 million in one year!

A Personal Message From the Author

Thank you for purchasing this book. I hope it was inspiring and insightful.

If you liked it, please be generous and give me the gift of a review. It doesn't have to be glowing, only genuine and fair.

Follow this link to easily post your review in less than 1 minute!

http://trk.as/ymsp

I heartily thank you,

Barry Powell

Contact me at: barrypowellbooks@gmail.com
Author Page: www.amazon.com/author/barrypowell

Made in the USA
Lexington, KY
09 July 2017